# Nobody's Hell

# Nobody's Hell

## Douglas Goetsch

Hanging Loose Press
Brooklyn, New York

Published by Hanging Loose Press, 231 Wyckoff Street, Brooklyn, NY 11217-2208. All rights reserved. No part of this book may be reproduced without the publisher's written permission, except for brief quotations in reviews.

Printed in the United States of America
10 9 8 7 6 5 4 3 2

Hanging Loose Press thanks the Literature Program of the New York State Council on the Arts for a grant in support of the publication of this book.

Cover art by Ed Fausty ◆ Cover design by Caroline Drabik

Acknowledgments: Many thanks to the journals where poems from this book first appeared: *Atlanta Review, Chiron Review, Folio, Graffiti Rag, Hanging Loose, The Hampden-Sydney Review, The Iowa Review, The Ledge, The Marlboro Review, Mudfish, Nimrod, Prairie Schooner, Quarterly West,* and *Slipstream.* "Counting" and "Bachelor Song" were reprinted in *PoetryDaily.* Some poems in this book first appeared in *Wherever You Want,* Pavement Press Chapbook Award, 1997.

Thanks to the New York Foundation for the Arts for an artist's fellowship that helped make this book possible.

Thanks to fellow writers, friends and teachers who have made these poems, and this life, better: Kathy Collins, Susan Pliner, Brigit Pegeen Kelly, Robert McDowell, Jill Hoffman, Judith Kocela Hawk, Ken Rosen, Alvaro Cardona-Hine, Marie Howe, Patricia Smith, Tim Seibles, Arthur Fredric, Lisa Denton, Angelo Verga, Barbara Tran, Margaret Burton, Ginger Andrews, Sherry Grimm,

Library of Congress Cataloging-in-Publication Data
Goetsch, Douglas.
    Nobody's hell / Douglas Goetsch.
        p.  cm.
    ISBN 1-882413-61-X. — ISBN 1-882413-60-1 (pbk.)
    1. City and town life—New York (State)—New York—poetry.
    2. Suburban life—New York (State)—Long Island—Poetry.  I. Title.
PS3556.03326N63    1998
811'.54—dc21                                    98-47420
                                                    CIP

Produced at The Print Center, Inc., 225 Varick St., New York, NY 10014, a non-profit facility for literary and arts-related publications. (212) 206-8465

# TABLE OF CONTENTS

*for Gladys Gordon*

# Counting

I'd walk close to buildings counting
bricks, run my finger in the grout
till it grew hot and numb. Bricks
in a row, rows on a floor, multiply
floors, buildings, blocks in the city.
I knew there were numbers for everything—
tires piled in mountains at the dump,
cars on the interstate to Maine,
pine needles blanketing the shoulder of the road,
bubbles in my white summer spit.
I dreamed of counting the galaxies
of freckles on Laura MacNally,
touching each one—*she loves me,*
*she loves me not*—right on up her leg,
my pulse beating away at the sea
wall of my skin, my breath
inhaling *odd,* exhaling *even.*

To know certain numbers
would be like standing next to God,
a *counting* God, too busy
to stop for war or famine.
I'd go out under the night sky
to search for Him up there:
God counting, next to Orion
drawing his bow. I'd seen
an orthodox Jew on the subway,
bobbing into the black volume
in his palms, mouthing words
with fury and precision, a single
drop of spittle at the center
of his lip catching the other lip

and stretching like silk thread.
At night I dreamed a constant stream
of numbers shooting past my eyes so fast
all I could do was whisper as they
came. I'd wake up reading the red
flesh of my lids, my tongue
flapping like ticker tape.

I come from a family of counters;
my brother had 41 cavities in 20 teeth
and he told everyone he met;
Grandpa figured his compound
daily interest in the den, at dusk,
the lights turned off, the ice
crackling in his bourbon; my father
hunched over his desk working
overtime for the insurance company,
using numbers to predict
when men were going to die.

When I saw the tenth digit added
to the giant odometer in Times Square
tracking world population, I wondered
what it would take for those wheels
to stop and reverse. What monsoon
or earthquake could fill graves faster
than babies wriggled out of wombs?
Those vast cemeteries in Queens—
white tablets lined up like dominoes
running over hills in perfect rows—
which was higher, the number
of the living or the dead? Was it
true, what a teacher had said:
get everyone in China to stand on a bucket,
jump at exactly the same time

and it'd knock us out of orbit?
You wouldn't need *every*one,
just enough, the right number,
and if you knew that number
you could point to a skinny
copper-colored kid and say
*You're the one, you can send us flying.*
That's all any child wants: to count.

That's all I wanted to be, the millionth
customer, the billionth burger sold, the one
with the foul ball, waving for TV.

I

# Dark Morning

Mom woke me. Power was out.
She handed me a flashlight. *Go
in the bathroom and shine it on him.*
He stood there, his face lit
by cream. I watched his strokes,
how he fingered his chin, glided the blade
past his jaw, turned the faucet on and off
to rinse it clean and bloodless,
the space between us wordless,
just the chuff-chuffing on his sandy face,
a face I can't ever remember touching,
and the stinging smell of menthol.

## Mrs. Britt's

She wore her black hair twisted around chopsticks, or braided in a rope to her waist. She didn't seem to care if she was fat, and her name was Barbara, but Mom didn't want us calling her that. I wanted Mrs. Britt for a mom.

They disappeared inside to talk about Dad, leaving Andy and me in the backyard with hula hoops that leaked dirty water, a kiddie pool full of soot, a rusted pogo stick that shrieked. Sometimes Jessica, their olive-skinned adopted child, came out to squat on her plastic potty, amber pee trickling from the fold in her crotch. From the back edge of the property you could see the Smithtown dump, where junked cars lined the sides of a ravine, tires strewn around them like fish eggs.

Grown-ups take a drug that keeps them talking for hours while children age outside. Mr. Britt, Deer Park High's wrestling coach, drove up in his Toyota, got out and chased us down. "Oh no!" he hollered, hands on the pressure points in our knees, "Not the Indian Deathlock!"

We screamed, "No!"

"You're right Barbara," said Mom, poking her head out the window, "it's Bill."

It was almost dark when they appeared on the back stoop. Mrs. Britt urged Mom to stay for another cup of coffee. Mom said his train would be there any minute. "He can wait!" Mrs. Britt said, stepping on her cigarette and twisting.

But Mom sped. First to Carvel's, so we wouldn't tell Dad where she'd been, then to the station. When the train pulled in she started the car, pushed the driver's seat all the way back and slid over to the passenger side. Schools of men in suits and briefcases came out of the dark and steam. One of them opened the door, got in, the car sinking with his weight, and drove us home.

# Easy

When Mom screwed up the courage she drove to Bohack's and came back with a dozen bags of groceries. Still, she feared we'd run out before the week was up. And we did, because those bags were filled with junk—candy, marshmallows, gallons of soda. No milk, no eggs, not a vegetable in sight.

Most nights we'd get take-out. At Young's China House they let me stand on a chair to see over the high counter, men in white, hovering in smoke, tossing dark wet food.

One morning I found Mom at the kitchen table with a shiny bald man in a suit. He was asking her questions about food, and filling out a long form. "Can you use chicken? Quartered? Whole? Gizzards?" Every so often Mom brought her hand to her mouth as if suppressing a cry. The man, who I would later know as George, touched her shoulder and said, "Easy, Carol."

When I came home from school there was a large white freezer, the kind that sits horizontal like a coffin, in our garage. A truck pulled up to fill it with frozen steaks, lamb chops, chickens whole and quartered, hamburger patties, breakfast sausage, bacon, waffles, French toast, orange juice concentrate, cut corn, pearl onions and creamed spinach in boil bags. I called Mom to the garage—they needed her initials—but she screamed from inside for me to sign.

The hour before Dad came home from work and asked for dinner, I heard steps in the garage. I stood at the door watching Mom, barefoot in her housedress, stare into the open freezer, vapor rolling out the sides and down her legs.

# Self-Portrait with Radio

*after Larry Levis*


A blue plastic radio on the table
by the bed, so cheap and small
it could barely stand on the side
it was meant to. But a child
doesn't know there's anything better
than static, as he turns the knob listening
for the Yankee game, glimpsed
as though through fog from a circling plane.
He sees it all in the voice of Phil Rizzuto—
this was before Scooter went senile,
announcing birthdays and anniversaries
of Italians he'd met in airports during
full counts with men on base,
before every male in New York City
wanted him put to pasture. But a child
doesn't know it's only the thin voice
of a frail man. He sees a game.
He sees Bert Campanaris of the Oakland A's
lay down a suicide squeeze in the ninth.
The bunted ball trickles out his wallpaper
onto his blanket. He tries to grab it,
flip it to Thurman Munson in time,
but all he gets is moonlight, and his Yankees
go three up three down to lose, and he sulks
in the night beside his radio despising
the commercial for AAMCO transmissions,
that stupid double-honk they use
to spell out the two A's in AAMCO.
Soon he'll know real disaster—his grandma
will drown in her own lungs, etc.—

but at the beginning of it all
was the Yankees losing, falling
a game further out of first, and nothing
could make the world bearable
until the next night, when they'd play again,
and Rizzuto's voice would be lit up like neon,
as if no bad thing could ever happen.
Late in the game he'll play it low,
so his parents, who've come to their bed
to argue, have sex and sleep, cannot hear
him, his radio, his struggle for happiness.

## Pig's Lungs

They only called it a dissection.
We lined up behind Miss Young,
she passed out straws, and one by one
we stepped up to the tray of lungs,
each the size of one of our torsos—
purplish brown, stiff, stale smelling—
stuck a straw into a sinewy hole
and blew. Bubbles rose, swelling
pink with life. We shoved Melanie
Shulman to the back—nobody
wanted to share a lung with her,
whose breath we were
more scared of than the pig's
going up our mouths, into our chests.

# Rice

I didn't know rice until I traded places with Rusty and went next door to eat. Rusty had a real mom who put her hair up in a bun and used all four burners of the stove. We, on the other hand, had chuck steak every night, the meat lined up like ammunition in the garage freezer. Mom pried it unstuck from its styrofoam tray with a bread knife.

But that's what Rusty wanted—steak—so while he watched my dad saw out the juicy strip down the middle, the only part not riddled with sinew, and haul it onto his own plate like a prize, I sat next door eating Mrs. Grimes's celestial rice—plump, saffron yellow, just a little crunchy—and listened to Mr. Grimes complain of Rusty's poor grades. Why couldn't he get straight A's like me, his dad wanted to know. Mrs. Grimes never said a word, never even asked about the meal, which was delicious. The two older sons, Tony, who pumped gas, and Donny, unemployed, kept their eyes down as they ate.

It didn't take Rusty long to wise up to the fact that he'd never get a decent piece of steak at my house, and Mom's Minute Rice was shredded cardboard, so pretty soon we were both eating at his house. Mr. Grimes still quizzed me on why Rusty was failing so miserably, but I didn't answer. Rusty could kick the shit out of me. He was no bigger than me, and a year younger, but he took me every time.

"You see, Russell?" his father said, pointing with his wet fork, "how Douglas studies and applies himself—"

"—But I *never* study," I said.

It was true, and I thought it would help, because Rusty didn't study either. Then we all realized it was more like calling him an idiot. Mrs. Grimes looked over at her husband and cleared her throat. Rusty just hung his head, like his brothers, and chewed his mother's rice.

# Ferrymen

*for Ely Silverman*


The parents in our town ferried us
back and forth to Cub Scouts, soccer,
Little League, and later, our first dates.
We loved to ride with Mr. Silverman,
who'd speak to us in his gentle baritone,
sometimes about the war, sometimes about
his lonely years single in Manhattan,
then meeting Alice, and, in his mid-forties,
a son he never expected, a new life…
though we could see the old life in him
when he took the school speed bumps at full speed,
and clocked in at seventy down Elwood Road.
He used to drive a cab, and his only wish
was to fly ahead to the next red light.

Mothers pruning roses on Highland Avenue
stood back startled at the beige Dodge Dart
tearing up the street. Inside we sat
crowded, plastered to the seat, our palms
upturned on our heads to cushion blows.
Sometimes Mr. Silverman would turn to us
and say, "So how the hell are ya?"
He'd really want to know, but when we felt
the queasy change in pressure in our bowels
with every rolling hill on Stanton Street,
we had no mouths to tell him how we were,
though Karl Blessing managed to squeak,
"I think you passed my house."
"So I did," crooned Mr. Silverman,
shoved it in reverse and floored it.

When you stepped into a car you stepped
into the good or bad weather of a family.
You'd breathe the smells of old unbathed dogs,
of french fries two weeks under the seat,
you'd see short gray hairs and dandruff
shed into the corners of the dash,
and you'd hear Mrs. Scott reminding Joe
nastily, in front of all his friends,
of the chores awaiting him when he got home.
Somewhere in life a young woman
became Mrs. Scott, and learned to love
the droning of her voice. We glanced at Joe,
at one another, knowing there was no
accounting for the differences in the souls
of our parents—the Mrs. Scotts and Mr. Silvermans
of this world—just as you didn't ask why
the good witch was good and the bad bad.

## Isn't That Beautiful

When I opened my eyes
we were halfway to Maine,
my brother's feet lying by
my head, my feet by his head
in the back of our Buick LeSabre.
Mom in the passenger seat,
her hair tied back in a scarf,
her forehead—what she used
to check for fever, pressing it
to ours—a wrinkle-free curve,
a full-blown sail, above
thick black-rimmed glasses.
*I loved you, Mom. I thought*
*you were the best of all possible*
*mothers. I used to ride my bicycle*
*down Malvern Lane, counting*
*the houses containing mothers*
*not as good as you.*
Sitting up, I saw Dad's hand
at the top of the wheel
spread wide from thumb to pinkie,
the littlest tip of his loafer
on the edge of the gas pedal—
how he could get such power
from our V-8 engine with that
corner of his big toe.
In the White Mountains, Mom
said, "Oh *isn't* that beautiful!"
whenever a turn in the road
revealed snowcapped peaks.
"*Isn't* that beautiful!"—when she saw
a moose, a covered bridge, a river

through birches. Breathless wonder
that came all the way from her
childhood in Brooklyn, hedged in
by thick slabs of brownstones.
We teased her from the back
in Edith Bunker falsetto:
"Oh *isn't* that beautiful!"
Dad, a hand on her knee, said
"Don't mock your mother."

## The Walls

In the suburbs our lives were separated
by sheetrock, which cracked like an egg
when you threw your brother into it.
The house was made entirely of chalk.
You'd walk through it, almost by accident
like a ghost. So when we heard the thump,
followed by the sound of falling chips,
we knew it was only Andy, who'd been poking
around the attic when the ceiling busted
through, depositing him in the bathtub
dusted white, confused, like a dumb idea
that couldn't even stay up in the head.

# Nobody's Hell

At the bus stop on the first frigid
morning in January I felt the prickle
of hairs freezing in the caves of my nostrils
each time I inhaled, and when Cathy
Stegbauer arrived having just showered,
I broke off pieces of her frozen curls.
Later in math class I studied her head
thawing into a ragged mop, the torn
curtain of bangs framing her face.
I pressed my reddened fingertips together
waiting for that warm tingle of feeling—
I was always petrified of frostbite,
of pieces of me never coming back,
like the brown zones in freezer-burned meat,
like a troubled memory where part
of the heart dies, like when Chris Paffle
dropped a penny on the locker room floor
and said to me, "Pick it up, Jew"—
I didn't believe this actually happened
because a piece of me froze right there.
It dangled in the center of me like a clapper
in a bell, like the diseased hamster
Dad put to sleep in the freezer; if it ever
defrosted it would smell like a murky river,
a place downwind of a nastier place.
In college, when I read Dante, I already
knew why the Inferno's core was frozen,
and why, coming up from that hole,
the first thing Dante gazed at was the stars—
someplace warm, someplace that is nobody's hell.

# Splendor

When I was fourteen reading *Rebecca*
I thought *That's me* not Rebecca
but someone with a place like Manderly
up a long winding neck of a road
through trees to a mansion the sea
a boathouse below and waves blowing
in the relentless wind like Beethoven.
I didn't know how I'd ever own this
place where the money would come from
to pay servants or win the woman
to bring here to live with me
or the other woman to be my mistress
and never mind all the trouble later—
the decadence the ruin the decay
I could take because I already knew
the beauty of sadness watching
Natalie Wood in *Splendor in the Grass*
on the 4:30 movie. How achingly perfect
and sunfilled and then how abruptly
photographs fade and we are old
which always seemed to happen
on the 4:30 movie—
*Summer of '42*
*Days of Wine and Roses*
*The French Lieutenant's Woman*—
the credits rolling the darkness gathering
in the trees outside where you couldn't get me
to play because I just wanted to dream
and sink into the couch where I
sometimes found Mom crying
with a Reader's Digest Condensed Book
in her hands and once crying

with nothing in her hands at all.
After the movie I sat back in the dark
wondering hard about the future
which aside from someplace vast sad windy
by the sea was as blank as the green glass
of the shut off Magnavox.

## The Beach

While they met with the real estate brokers,
Timmy Jones, the older boy next door,
took me down the slope. The sand was sharp
with stones and barnacles and vacant shells.
In tide pools hermit crabs lifted their
borrowed homes and dashed about like
old men caught in public in their underwear.
Sea gulls tore away at mussel beds,
hoisting them up, teetering on stiff wings,
then dropping and cracking shells on rock.
He pointed to the stripes of stiffened seaweed:
the high-water mark, receding.
In the salt stink of muck at low tide
I wondered why my parents wanted this.

Later, the beach was always good for hiding
when stores phoned to say I'd shoplifted.
Later, I went there for teenage brooding—
I thought the incoming waves proved
something about time, how every moment
carries the next on its back. Timmy stole
our wood for bonfires. I spied on them
partying, drinking, getting to third base.
A month before he left, Dad sat down there
in the June sun, on a blanket, with a lady,
in plain sight of Mom, up at the house
drying dishes. She told us it was only
Mrs. Kaufman, Dad's new bridge partner.
They were going over bids, strategies.

# Northport

The girl who fucked was Margaret Pritchard.
She was tall, lemon blonde and pretty
damn near perfect, a walking statue
past the rows of textbooks piled
in our laps, solemn in her make-up
on her way to the back of the bus
where they smoked. In the school play
she was Sarah Brown, the holy woman
with the Save-A-Soul mission.
Sky Masterson took her to Havana,
got her drunk, the curtain closed
and Margaret disappeared, leaving
her much less pretty sister, Catherine,
and rumors. The one I believed
involved the man in the white mansion
at the top of Ocean Avenue, behind
the high hedge and wrought iron gate,
set back a hundred yards by a driveway,
a house that seemed to say,
*Haunt me with your rumors.*
*We are strange, we don't go in public,*
*you don't even know our names—*
*the postman barely does—and all*
*of it, whatever you say, is so.*
The red car on the side lawn
with long Cadillac fins, was also a boat—
I know you don't believe this
but it's true, I'd actually seen it
cruising on the bay. Maybe
when Margaret fucked the man
they took off in that car, drove it
over the Long Island Sound

to Connecticut, glittering at dusk
on the horizon. I heard all you
needed was twenty miles out to sea
for the curve of the Earth to hide you.
If so, they were home free, somewhere
beyond that curve, living. We were
home in Northport, virgins, getting
good grades, staying out of rumors.

# Ronny

During a heart attack, my favorite uncle
explained, part of the heart muscle dies.
I tried to picture that dead patch in him,
purplish-gray and stiffened, shaped
maybe like the ink spot on Jupiter.
Then in a flash I saw him riding his heart
like a rodeo cowboy, the living portion
bucking up and down in bright red spasms.

At Jones Beach I used to ride his back
into deep water. Mother said he brought me
for the women, who stopped at our towels
to admire my platinum blond hair.
He lived with us that summer, home
from Viet Nam, via Saigon, via Las Vegas,
carrying his wife's Dear John letter,
and just enough money for a used Camaro.

# Walking Wounded

*for Stephen Dobyns*


Spring came and we had to hide our boners
under our desks or against walls of lockers.

We'd see other boys walking with books slung low
and we'd know. Sometimes I'd have a hand in my pocket

pulling it down and to the side—it swelled and jacked itself up
altogether on its own, as a big dog climbs your sweater

trying to hump you, its own stupid boner, telescoped
like lipstick, brushing your thigh. Boners

as girls came up the stairs, glossy-lipped
in knit dresses, slim-hipped in tight jeans

as boys descended weirdly, like that wounded
fife player from the American Revolution.

In the bathroom poor Richie Kearns
was trying to get it down, talking to it—

*Damn you!* I thought I heard him mutter—
and flicking at it—not to punish, just deter,

as your dad whacks you in the neck
from across the dinner table.

At night was when we got the good ones
that came with thoughts of slipping ourselves

into Sarah, Margie, Barbara, Nancy, Elisa.
We said their names, repeating some, to see

who got us stiffest. Afterwards, we worried they
would leave us when we most needed them: in the presence

of a girl at night in the park or by the docks.
Would she be the kind who'd say *Maybe,* and *Not yet,*

until you whimpered and shrank back into yourself?
Or would she make you long and fat

and firm as cement, tell you it was good
and big, while she stroked and licked it?

# Lawyer

In the outer office, there were mossy rugs with coffee stains. Mom knitted. I stared at the stockinged calves of secretaries, rolling chairs on plastic sheets.

After two hours Jack came out. Black horn-rimmed glasses, black sideburns, wide hungry jaws. He said, "Come in, Carol," all buttery, kissing her cheek. He said, "No calls, no disturbances."

Mom said, "Jack, meet my son."

Jack shook my hand. He turned back to Mom and said, "Are you sure you want him here for this?"

"You don't know my son," said Mom.

Jack started asking questions. Mom told him she and Dad had had a "good" sex life. I pictured her down on him like a slave, little wet slapping sounds coming from her mouth.

Jack said, "How likely is he to remarry?"

"*That bitch*? Don't make me laugh." Mom leaned forward. "You see, Kent has a thing for bottoms. He simply needs a woman to have one, and Sylvia...well, she's got nothing." She sat back and smiled, the first time in weeks.

Jack looked at me. His glasses had slipped to where his nose got fat.

Later, he wrote down a figure and handed it to her. She smiled again, showing all the tartar on her teeth.

# Jack Nicklaus

My father follows Jack Nicklaus.
He follows him into the rough,
the woods, over footbridges,
wherever Nicklaus hits his ball.
He tries not to admit it
but he knows he is watching
a beautiful man, taller than he is
with golden hair.
His caddy, Jack Nicklaus, Jr.
is taller than both.
Late in the day, he begins to
call him Jack. "Go Jack!"
he shouts, as the tee shot soars.
My father is vice president
of an insurance company;
he has never said Go
Anyone in his life, but this
is Nicklaus, the Golden Bear,
now hunched in his putting stance,
stiff and stately as a grandfather clock.
Just before the pendulum swings,
he rises. He takes
a few steps toward the gallery,
points to my father, who can hardly
believe Nicklaus's blue eyes
meeting his, and in that moment
what do my father's eyes say—
*Jack, how do I get my sons to like me?*
But it is only a moment,
followed by the next, where Nicklaus
puts his finger to his lips
and says, "Shh."

# Gay

Margie was a sprinter, fastest girl
in the county. She always wore pants,
the belt slung low on her hips.
My friends said she had a guy's ass—
squarish, nothing but packed muscle.
But I saw the tiny sway in her walk,
the way the wrinkles in her corduroys switched
sides. There was, for me, more in this
than in the swelling breasts of cheerleaders.
In the movie theater she grabbed my hand.
No words, no quickened breaths, just
the fever of her fingers wrapping mine.
Out in Larkfield Park she shot
her thin tongue in my mouth.

One day I heard about a fight
at Margie's house. Her older brother
told the family he was gay
and they kicked him out. Margie never
spoke about it, but this brother
made her more sexy to me than ever.
The next week we broke up.
She was waiting outside my physics class
in a skirt. A tweed skirt, stockings
and heels. We walked to a window
where light poured in—it had just turned spring.
"Are you sure," I said,
staring at the shine on her
stockings. "Are you sure?"

## Standing Up Stiff

When I told Mom I hated her
she was in the kitchen,
I was sitting at Dad's desk,
the desk she moved
from his study to the living room,
when Dad moved out.

Dad used to sit with
his feet up on the desk
flying the flag of his cigarette
as he went over the rules for talking—
she was not to be redundant,
she was not to ramble on,
she was to stick to the point
which was why the hell couldn't she
get anything done from the list,
like renew the car registration,
spay the dog,
pick up his clubs, re-gripped and waiting
five goddamn weeks already.
Mom embarked on explanations
but Dad nipped them in the bud,
saying *Carol, the rules!*
Mom saying *How can you know
what I'm about to say?*
Back and forth like this
till way past dinner
and she'd drive out for Eddie's Pizza
which came back puddled with oil.

Moving the desk was part
of making the house her own,

which meant letting the dog piss and shit everywhere—
no more waking before Dad
rushing around with bunched paper towels—
which meant her new friends,
Parents Without Partners,
coming over any time they wanted
to circle chairs and bitch
about all those years married to Uptight.
Later they got drunk, put on Neil Diamond.
The women let the men feel them up
before smacking them for getting fresh.
No one seemed to mind
the smell of dog piss, sharpest
in the corner of the den
where I was sitting, at Dad's desk,

the day I said *I hate you, Mom,*
then added *I really do hate you.*
Not a sound from the kitchen,
but I knew where she was—
at the open refrigerator—
and I could picture the auburn hairs of her moustache
standing up stiff.

## Wherever You Want

When I said fuck you to my father for not paying child support like the judge ordered, we were at his bachelor pad in Smithtown, a wing of a house which looked out on a backyard swimming pool where somebody's kids were playing. He offered me a ride home, but I slammed the door and started walking. When he drove up alongside me I gave him the finger, held it up like a torch, until he finally peeled away, leaving me alone for the walk. Ten miles. I liked it.

I went on walks all summer, out Elwood Road past my high school, past the next town's high school, walking the shoulder at dusk, headlights streaking across my eyes as I tried for perfect steps, absorbing shocks with my ankles, knees, hips, so that my head floated on top of me as though dangling from the heavens by a silk thread. I walked Jericho Turnpike, miles of car dealers, furniture showrooms, funeral homes, strip malls, broken glass. I stopped at the sign for The Tender Trap, the letters pink and black, tall as me. I'd passed it hundreds of times in the car with Mom.

The fat guy at the door didn't even card me, just took my three bucks and said, "Enjoy yourself, son." I stepped through a curtain of black rubber slats like you find in a car wash. A woman was kneeling on the bar, circling her hips in the face of a bald guy who looked like Mr. Damuelowitz, my Little League coach. I took a seat at the other end. I tried to signal the bartender to order a drink. Instead, the stripper—though not *technically* a stripper because she had no clothes to take off—got up and headed over, cellulite jiggling on her legs, men lifting their heads sheepishly as she passed. She stopped in front of me, crouched down, opened her thighs, rocked her torso forward and back, forward and back like a nauseous reflection in a doorknob. She smelled a little rubbery, a little like Mom, breasts pointing down at me like tired accusations.

Another time I kicked a bottle cap down 25A, which banked around hills by the harbor, then turned inland at the Charcoal Cottage, where Mom had passed out the year before after two sips of a Southern Comfort Sour. Dad told everyone to just let her lie there until she came to. But I threatened the manager, who called the paramedics, who swore Mom had the lowest blood pressure on record. We watched them work on her, then strap her onto a gurney and drive off. A year later Dad left in the night. His train station car, the Gremlin, with all those blue *New York Times* delivery bags in the back, became his get-away car. He drove to the Commack Motor Inn for his rendezvous with Mrs. Kaufman, and they each phoned to call off their marriages. Next day at noon Dad drove up in the Gremlin. He'd come for the pictures of ships in his study, marching back and forth through the bedroom, where Mom still had the covers over her head, swearing she'd lie there until she died.

I'd been kicking the same bottle cap for miles, through North-port, Centerport, Greenlawn, into Huntington, where the Galaxy Diner sat wrapped like a birthday present in shining chrome, its neon sign blazing *OPEN ALL NIGHT.* I gazed at the cakes and pies in the revolving case, the toppings piled high and stiff like the old waitress's hair. "Wherever you want," she said. I was the only customer. I sank into a cushioned booth and ordered coffee and lemon meringue pie. Mom could make about three things well, and lemon meringue pie was one of them. I used to stand on a chair next to her as she gently tossed the yolks from shell to shell over a glass bowl. Just the littlest bit of yolk, she said, would contaminate the whites and they would never rise. She poured in sugar, a teaspoon of vanilla and got out the mixer. I watched the amber puddle climb the sides of the bowl, turning pure white—how could so much come from so little, I wondered. She spread the meringue thick over lemon filling, making peaks and tufts with the edge of the spatula, which I would soon get to lick. In the Galaxy Diner, miles from home, I spackled each forkful of pie onto the roof of my mouth, licked it down, let some of it turn to juice, smeared the rest back up again, and again, until it all dissolved.

**II**

## Such a Good Dancer

Desperate to be part of the night,
we jerked like a bunch of spazzes
to that screaming eunuch, Michael Jackson.
Randi Muelbach kept remarking
*You're such a good dancer!*
drawing closer, letting me grab her
saggy ass. My boogying was a sort
of two-step hip gyration while holding
my plastic cup of grain alcohol level.
I had perfected the arm that remained still,
kept it out like a bird feeder. Randi
glued elbows to waist and swung
forearms, hands and hips furiously.
She was sweating something fierce.
Her perfume was foul swamp flowers.

From the futon on her floor I watched
her pull her dress over her head.
Fat and sadly flat-chested,
legs already bluing with veins, thick
knees knocked in, the way the back
wheels of a Volkswagen buckle with a load.
Disgusted with myself—two years
in college and still a virgin—I would
stick my dick in a girl and end that.
As she stepped out of her underwear
I said, *After tonight I don't want us
to ever talk again. OK?*
That's what I said.
She looked down at me and said
*Sure,* like it was nothing.

Through the cinder block walls
I could hear that whole dorm writhing
on a Saturday night. Even Kim Putnam,
the born-again who wore only long skirts
and was losing her hair, was getting banged
and moaning like a wild woman.
Sometimes it sounded like a crowd
ooh-ing and ahh-ing at a car accident;
sometimes I heard the night as one fuck
xeroxed and traveling room to room
like a rumor, or luck—good or bad—
either way, I wriggled and fought
on top of Randi Muelbach,
who kept whispering in my ear
*Such a good dancer.*

## Naples

You come out the maze of alleys by the sea.
They are selling tripe, sprinkled with lemon
and salt. You ask the time, find out later
he lied. You get on a bus. Swaying
in the aisle is a gigantic transvestite
with a face like John Wayne.
He says, *Bella Napoli.* A man
tells you the restaurant you want
on the *Posillipo* is still open.
You get off, find out he lied.
You see him laughing from the balcony
of his Fascist building. *Hai fame, Americano?*
he says, waving you up.

Five ugly sisters lean on their elbows
and stare. Half of Naples, it occurs
to you, has those same crossed eyes,
so you think about incest.
They keep asking *Are you rich?*
Mama serves you pasta with bacon.
They call *Il Nonno* to the table
for dirty jokes. He barks
his lines in dialect, something about
a finger and a phone. You worry
he'll spit out a rotten tooth. He
pokes you in the chest to see if you get it.
The sisters poke you to help you get it.
Mama yells *Ma che stronzo!*—calling you
bird shit—and you just sit there mopping
up sauce with your bread. Delicious.

## Looking for an Apartment

I suppose I could go on living on Chinese food—
Sweet and Sour Pork, $6.95—
flirting with the waitresses,
getting them to stand blushing side by side
so I can guess which sister is older.
I'll marry you both, I tell them. (They probably hate me.)
We will have thousands of children.

I've been drifting down streets, examining faces,
trying to guess their rent. (I love to say "rent-poor.")
There really isn't much to my huddled mass:
old T-shirts, yellowed books, baldness remedy,
the Citibank mug Grandma attached herself to just before
     dying.
Cold weather is good, I tell the broker—
walk in shivering, see if it feels like home.

# Three Blind Dates

### 1

She has chosen a beautiful Italian café,
marble tables shaped like apples
with bites taken out of them.
I sit by the window and watch
the women on MacDougal Street
as they come out of the law school
in suits with short skirts. Who will it be?
An hour goes by. Stood up.
At home, a message on the machine:
*This is Ros. I was the fat one*
*in the green dress. You walked in*
*and took a table by yourself.*
*You didn't even see me.*
*Thanks a lot.*


### 2

When she told me on the phone
she was a psychiatrist, I pictured
me telling her everything,
pouring my heart out
as I peeled the clothes
from her pale shoulders.
But she is nine inches taller
than me, with a horse's head
and large troubled eyes that stare out
and seem to say, *There are goldfish*
*swimming inside, can you help?*
Maybe you'll call, she says later,
trembling, folding
herself into a cab.

### 3

I say she seems nervous. She says no,
that she thinks she knows
herself a lot better than I do.
I look at her: a nose
that would disagree with any face.
The waitress is gorgeous.
When she comes over I tell her
we are admiring her arms, long and muscled,
sleeves rolled to the shoulders.
Yes, she used to work out. My date
stands up: I am the most presumptuous man
she has met so far. What's more
she's sorry she told me about her family,
all those relatives in concentration camps.

# Not My Life

Her name was Lisa, the fourth
Lisa I had met. My phone
was ringing off the hook with
Lisa. This one was an editor
of wedding videos in Secaucus.
Lisa wanted babies. She wanted
babies and she wanted to get
married. She said this
from across the café table.
She was ready to spend
the rest of her life with me.
We tongue-kissed
in the Hoboken train station.
The autumn I turned thirty,

there always seemed to be
a young couple walking ahead
of me, arms draped about
necks and shoulders, fingers
slipped into back pockets.
What is it that lets people fit
into one another's lives? I don't
know, but in late November

I took a ferry to my third date
with Lisa. At five o'clock
the sun was already setting
behind the low cliffs of Weehawken.
An old clapboard house stood
up there in the cold wind,
framed against the sky,
the kind of house where you know

the loose boards whistle
all winter, the kind of house
that makes you want to cry
*Not here. This is not my life.*
*The sun isn't really*
*going down this early*
*and I don't love Lisa from New Jersey*
*and never will. I didn't love*
*the last Lisa or the one*
*before, and I knew it*
*as fast as it took to see that house*
*and know I will be old in a blink.*

# Andy

I'm sitting in this casino restaurant
surrounded by numbers,
long-legged girls strutting
around with Keno boards,
names like Hope and Lucky
tagged to their chests.

The cards have been god-awful.
I get aces full and this guy
catches his fourth jack
on the river. Second best
is worst you always say and
it's true enough for stud.

I haven't lost that much—
I could get it all back
in ten minutes of blackjack
and maybe I will.
I'm more worried about
you, still eating as though

you had a hole to fill,
and racing—70 m.p.h.
down Linden Avenue as you
explained your plan
to retire at 40 and die at 60.
Why is your life a contest?

Why can't it be a long day
where you forget time,
like when I ran away from home
and you followed me down
Nesconset Highway to where
the potato farms began?

We'd never gone that far on foot—
some places you never picture
being without parents. The sun
seemed to hang on the horizon
like it was nailed there.
Cars on the highway hit us

with walls of wind, drying
my tears as you caught up
and asked how much
was in the piggy bank I carried
under my arm like a football.
When I told you, you got me

back to Brothers' Trattoria
on Hallock Road, where we
spent my life savings on pizza—
I even paid for sausage on yours.
Seems like Mom and Dad never
got to see the good between us.

It's 2 a.m. I know you're still
awake, playing contract bridge
against a machine halfway
around the world, the computer
screen lighting your face blue.
Every ten minutes you check

stocks in Tokyo, and the west
coast ball games you bet on.
You yawn, crack the bones
in your neck, and think
about your eldest son
who has taken to shoplifting

as you once did. Sometimes
you stand at the door and watch
his face, hairless, asleep
and find it so hard to believe.
Andy, get some rest.
He'll probably be fine

in a few months. You're
a good person, in spite
of your temper, and the things
you used to say to make me
throw the television at you.
Remember when we sent

each other to the hospital,
one doctor pulling the pencil
lead out of my back, another
checking the gash in your leg
for whether I'd struck bone
with the fire iron? Hard

to believe I'd ever think
of you as good, especially
now that you resemble
Dad so much—right down
to his big gut and his Buick.
Hey, I'm about done with my

pie and coffee. There's
an hour before the next bus
and I guess I'll be on it.
First I'll stop at roulette
and play your favorite
numbers: 3, 13 and 33.

## Love in Vegas

I thought money was love when you
found me at the nickel slots and told me
you'd lost some, admitted later you'd
lost a lot, and that you wired New York
and lost that too. I joined you at blackjack,
where your last twenty held for two hours.
Women in sarongs fed us black Russians
until I lost count, and told them to hit me
when I already had 21, because
love is wanting what you already have,
I swore, as you howled, as we swayed
down the desert to our cheap hotel
and hit the bed in one another's arms.

# The Key

I have memorized the coastline
of your key, fingering it
in my pocket all morning.
One chink reminds me of the gap
in your teeth. Another, the space
between your first two toes.
This whole jagged ridge could be
your heartbeat on an EKG.

Lunch hour, I drive over,
slip it in your door,
sit in your closet, smell
your clothes, unbuckle, run
your silk between my legs,
lie on sheets we melted on
the night before, when you reached down
and whispered, *This belongs to me.*

## Mary

I promise not to touch you if we pull
the beds together, and you let your hair—
old cells, belonging as much to the world
as to you—drape across to me, so I might twist
it in my fingers as you do, in the fruit market
questioning yourself about melon and time
and the man who put you back on the pile
and made you never want to touch again.
If what they say is true—a woman's hair
grows seven years long before letting go—
I'd find the day he did it, a sad ripple
circling your head like a fallen halo,
and brush it out until it shone like new,
and lay it back upon you like a blanket.

## Living Alone

You take the homeless guy
for a cup of coffee—you've got time,
you want to see where your money goes.

You make friends with the dog
tied up outside the video store,
run your fingers
along the velvet folds of his forehead
until he doesn't want you to leave.

You love waitresses—
they always come back.

You still dream of the most
beautiful girl in high school,
the one at the center of the kickline.
You are playing chess
with her on an empty beach.
The sun is going down.
Your move.

You telephone the woman
you almost moved in with.
She is on a farm in Indiana,
her husband long gone.
You can hear the baby crying.

Life is next door. You smell the sauce
cooking as you climb the stairs.

## Partner

At 2 a.m. I rode the subway to Manhattan
to shoot pool with ruined men
who looked at you with bloodshot eyes
and said, *How 'bout another?*
Sure.
The tables were rectangular islands
of light, the balls spotted
and striped tropical birds.
Life wasn't perfect,
but here you could depend
on the straightness of the rails,
the solid crack of fake ivory,
the level plain of green.

Sometimes I played with a big country boy
who liked to pick fights with blacks.
He told folks to call him Tex
but I called him Ron
and he called me Partner.
I think he was a hit man—*Ah do
favors for paiple* was the way
he put it. One night we played
straight pool to 500. Long about
dawn, as I was crouching to shoot,
he stuck his massive hand before my eyes.
*See this?* It was a gold ring.
*Ah got married today.*

# Sleeping with Grandpa

Beneath king-size bedclothes
we lie on separate mattresses.
The fissure between them is a cold spot
where I love to wedge my foot.
He tries for slow, even breaths
but his body is full of farts and complaints.
He's been going to bed earlier each day,
rehearsing, hoping to be stolen away.

I get up to masturbate,
go through the living room,
out to the porch. Outside the screen
the Florida night is hot and thick.
I play the film: girl on the beach,
black triangle patch of her bikini ass
switching back and forth, back and forth
as she steps down to the water.

I come back to bed. He
is aware of my every move.
Once, I felt the mattress shake
in steady rhythm, but I thought
*No.* Now, he groans,
rolls away, and for a moment
I think the pulling sheet
is his loose skin.

## Midway

At least he knows when to get drunk,
plant elbows on the bar. Pretty soon
things please him, the song on the juke,
motion of the crowd against his back—
stones polishing one another. A guy
chews out his girl, every third word fuck.
An old man licks the Scotch he dribbled
down his arm. Thoughts come off shelves,
bright things that skitter through and die.
But one sticks: he is midway:
half the world is better off than him,
half worse.

# Urban Poem

We are made of newspaper and smoke.
We dunk roses in vats of blue.
The birds don't call—pigeons play it close
to the vest. When the moon is full
we hear it in the sirens. The Pleiades
you could probably buy downtown. Gravity
is the receiver on the hook. Mortality
we smell on certain people as they pass.

# Lay It Down

*for Brigit Pegeen Kelly*

Brigit, I took a bus through your state,
south, over those long elbows of rusted bridges,
over salt marshes, past oil tanks, train yards,
electric fields, past Matawan, Red Bank,
into the pine barrens, where the Garden
State Parkway feels like a low lane
through a hundred miles of hedges.
I got off and buried myself
among poker players in a windowless room
they pump with oxygen to keep us going.
Around the table, victims of a wreck:
fat woman with eczema scratching her forearms;
old man whose head won't stop jiggling;
tall guy in a Phillies cap with slots
in the pads of his fingers; Jewish lady
in a gold blouse, gold bracelets, five gold rings
and a smoker's voice that calls us
*Sweetheart.* The only name we know
is Mitch, here since Wednesday
the dealer tells us, tapping him awake.

Brigit, in another life I'd be like you,
busy with a child this first summer weekend,
walking the pasture, finding the lost calf,
hanging laundry. But I am not that person,
for reasons I seem to have no control over,
so I take the Special to Atlantic City
where old women pull slot machines
deep into the night, buckets of silver dollars
in laps where they once held children.

It's like a ride through the veins of a junkie
but it calms me, all this desire naked
as the waitress, who knows we're looking
sidelong at her bare back as she bends.
The old man stares into his losing hand,
ignoring calls to lay it down. Old wounds,
here we lick them deeper, getting up
only for the bathroom or more money.

Coming home, my uncle stopped in Vegas
with his soldier's pay, his wife gone,
his next wife two years away in a singles bar,
his third a dozen years behind her.
*It's all in the genes,* he said the other day
on the phone from the hotel where he lives.
I couldn't believe it: picked clean
by war, vetoed by his sons, saying
it was meant to be. Then I realized
why he could laugh: he'd fallen so far behind
he was ahead just by being alive.
I want to know what that's like.
Each spring I meet the woman
who will cancel out all previous women,
only to discover she doesn't like me
in the least, and I don't blame her.
June comes and boredom descends
on me like locusts. I get up and move

to blackjack, where they whoop and scream
as stacks of chips go up and down
like cities instantly built and demolished.
A bull-necked man is scared to take a hit
past twelve. I watch him lose $500
screaming for the dealer to break.
New staff comes on for the afternoon shift.

It's 95° outside, one tells me.
I could have quit with 95
but it's just a number, Brigit

and I'm out in the sun, walking in dust
past winos who stoop to check rolling paper bags
in the hot sea breeze, and the hotter breath
of buses pouring in from cities.
I cross avenues named for the states
of our country in no apparent order—
Michigan, Pennsylvania, Virginia, Kentucky—
names I knew as a child, playing Monopoly.
Up ahead, there's music—
organ, electric bass, then voices.
You can always tell a church full of black people
by the way the building wants to get up and fly.
An elegant man in a suit steps out
for a cigarette. He sees me, motions me
to go on in. I ask if it's OK
to stand there, which we both do,
watching how the wind through open doors
flaps dresses tight to limbs,
wraps around pews, up and down aisles
swift and solemn as the Holy Ghost.
They're mostly women, mouths wide,
heads tipped back, backs lurching
in a kind of violent agreement
with a wall of sound in five-part harmony.
*I don't know much about religion*
I tell the man, *but that sounds right.*

# A Haircut

Three old Jewish men sit ahead of Grandpa. One has a faded German accent. Grandpa taps me, points to a forearm, a tattooed number.

The three are given the same bad haircut. The barber has elaborate ways of taking off more and more. His scissors never stop chewing.

Grandpa's turn.

On top he is bald, except for a few dozen strands he keeps rock star long for combing back in a stripe. He hasn't seen a barber since he started on chemo. His doctor can't understand why it hasn't fallen out yet. "Harry," he finally said, "get a haircut."

Grandpa's hands grip the armrests.

*When I was fifteen, blond hair to my shoulders, we cut a deal: five dollars for one inch—no more. But he slipped the barber ten and told him to butcher me, which he did. I screamed in the car.*

I bring the car around. "Great haircut!" I say.

"Nonsense," he says getting in, "he took it all!"

He's right. There's even a little blood on his forehead where a mole used to be. Still, there is something boyish and handsome about his head.

"The women at the residence will be talking," I warn.

"Women," he says, batting his hand. "At my age all I can do is pat it and wish it well."

# Praise You Harry Gordon
### *(1906 - 1997)*


Praise you Harry Gordon
and your tie clips, cufflinks, trinkets of gold,
foreign coins and all those generations
of New York City subway tokens
in drawers with slots and finger-wide grooves,
curled brown photographs of ancestors in Europe
who told you who you were,
praise the walnut wood of your shoe trees
filling out Oxfords, Deerstags, Italian loafers,
black and blue leather soft as dogs' ears
loyally waiting for you to collect
jaywalking tickets from a hundred American cities
where you sold household pharmaceuticals
in airports and convention halls, shoving food
to the sides of your mouth to talk—
not once in forty years did you spit on a client—
telling numberless stories, none of them quite true,
of clubs where leggy waitresses swished by
carrying the best bourbon, prime rib
at the Gaslight, flanken at Lou Siegel's,
Pat Cooper in the Catskills
and the night your dice caught fire in Vegas
and Dean Martin came round to watch you roll—
he cheered for you, for you Harry!
Praise for your simple salesman's toast
and for when you put the champagne down
to take Grandma's face in both your hands
and plant a fat New Year's kiss
in your sloppy, small man's way of kissing.
Praise the custom blazers with your name

sewn into them, the pinkie ring
bought on a whim in Chicago,
the diamond brought home for her
half out of guilt for where you'd been
and the fun you'd had alone.
Then you retired, then she died, and you
tried to stuff in my valise, at the ends
of visits, one by one, all your things, right
down to your black mesh bikini underwear, thin as gauze.
Thirteen years, and then the hospital
where nurses bathed and turned your body
like muscled angels—the last one,
Evelyn, a beauty, actually stooping to kiss
lips you puckered days after
you'd had it with speaking or eating.
In the early morning I signed the release
of your body, along with the sheet
listing what you had when you phoned the taxi
and came to die:
shirt, shoes, trousers, underpants, teeth.

## Short Song

The self is a ship in a bottle.
You want to build it when you're young
but if not, no matter, the self
will be the thing in you that's sad
when the sun goes down. Ninety
percent of it you'll never know
but there are worse things to not know
like the rest of a song
the great Russian novels
or the way home.

# Bachelor Song

It's Saturday night and Lisa
is burying her husband
and me in Scrabble, long
words coming out of her
like children—theirs
are upstairs, finally asleep
at 9 o'clock, when Lisa's
speech slurs from exhaustion
and Arthur calls me Honey
by mistake. They wrestle
on the carpet in hysterics,
roll into a kiss.

The window in the guest room
douses the bed with moonlight.
I close my eyes picturing
Susan Sarandon in *Atlantic City*
bathing her chest with lemons.
Last night Nina phoned.
She's decided to stop dating.
She hasn't gotten over
Howard, and her hands
are full with her 5-year-old.
She asked about work, about
my poetry. I said, Listen
I feel fine: you're not dating
and I'm glad I was the man
who helped clear that up
for you. I'll never

get to sleep in this light.
Now I remember, it's the last
night of the new comet.
Hale-Bopp, two guys
who spent their lives looking
at the sky, found it.
They say it won't be back
for 2000 years. I don't
understand how a chunk of ice
holds together for that long,
leaving its comb of light
like a whistled song.